PIANO · VOCAL · GUITAR

KELLY CLARKSON
PIECE BY PIECE

ISBN 978-1-4950-2217-3

7777 W. BLUEMOUND RD. P.O. BOX 13819 MILWAUKEE, WI 53213

Visit Hal Leonard Online at
www.halleonard.com

HEARTBEAT SONG

Words and Music by JASON EVIGAN,
MITCH ALLAN, KARA DioGUARDI
and AUDRA MAE

Moderately fast

This is my heart-beat song_ and I'm_ gon-na play_ it. Been_ so long,_ I for-got _ how to turn_ it up,_ up, up,_ up all_ night long,_ oh, up,_ up all_ night long.

You, where the hell did you come from?_

mf

N.C.

Recorded a half step lower.

INVINCIBLE

Words and Music by WARREN FELDER,
STEVE MOSTYN, SIA FURLER
and JESSE SHATKIN

SOMEONE

Words and Music by
MATTHEW KOMA

TAKE YOU HIGH

Words and Music by JESSE SHATKIN
and MAUREEN McDONALD

Moderately

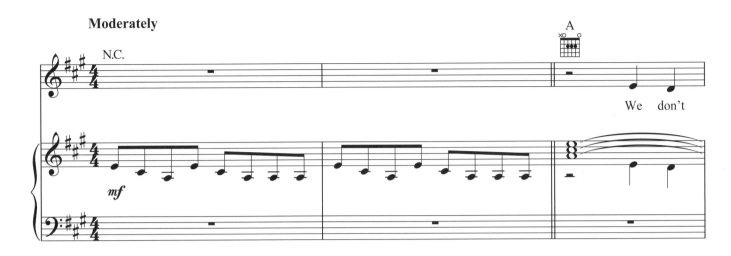

We don't

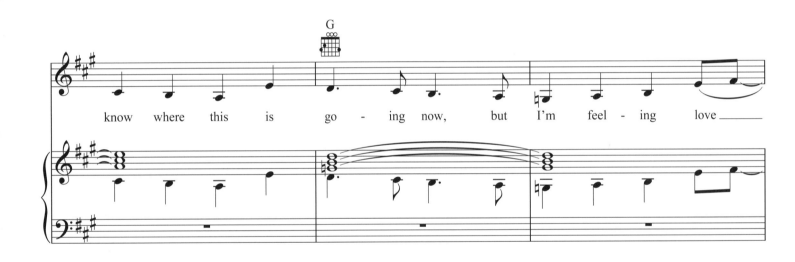

know where this is go-ing now, but I'm feel-ing love ___

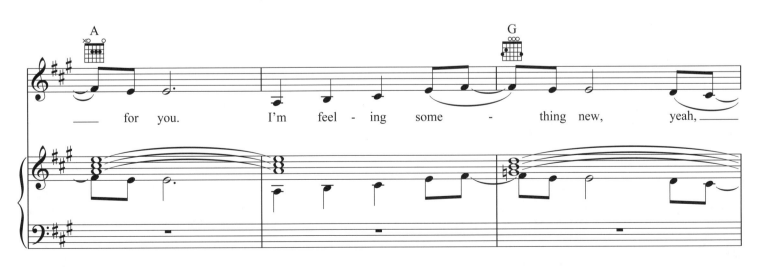

___ for you. I'm feel-ing some - thing new, yeah, ___

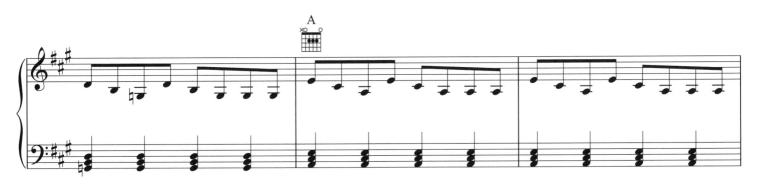

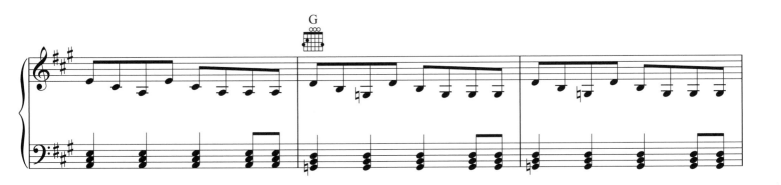

PIECE BY PIECE

Words and Music by KELLY CLARKSON
and GREG KURSTIN

Recorded a half step lower.

RUN RUN RUN

Words and Music by RY CUMING,
JOACIM PERSSON and DAVID JOST

I HAD A DREAM

Words and Music by KELLY CLARKSON
and GREG KURSTIN

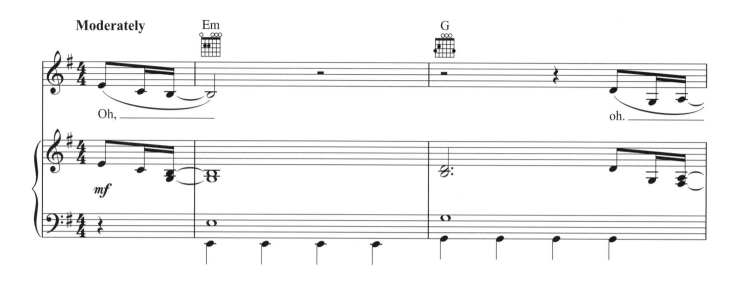

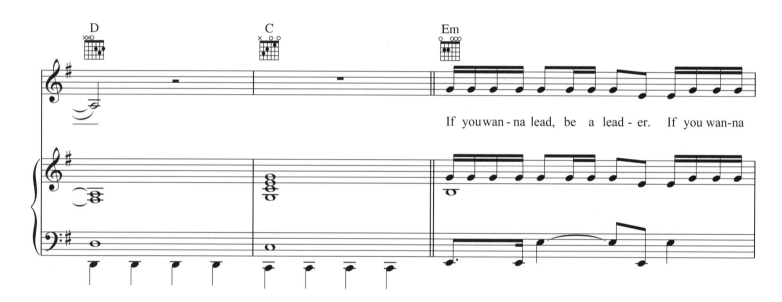

LET YOUR TEARS FALL

Words and Music by GREG KURSTIN
and SIA FURLER

TIGHTROPE

Words and Music by KELLY CLARKSON
and GREG KURSTIN

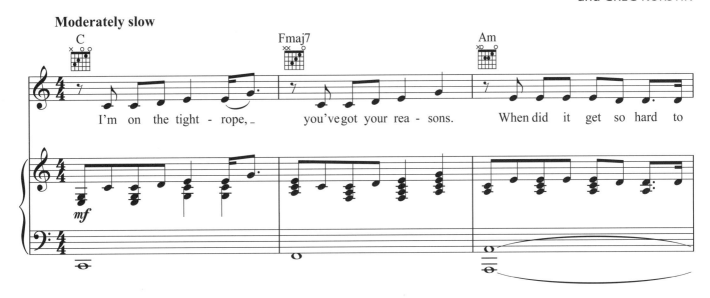

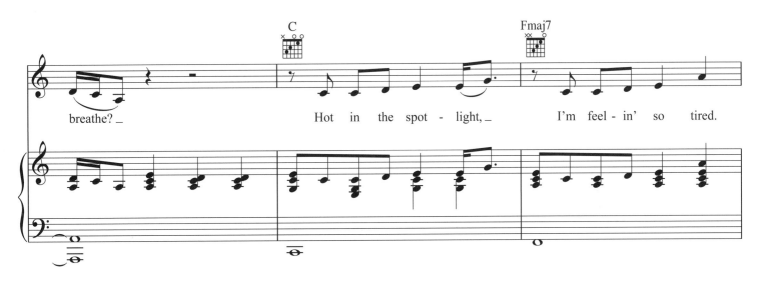

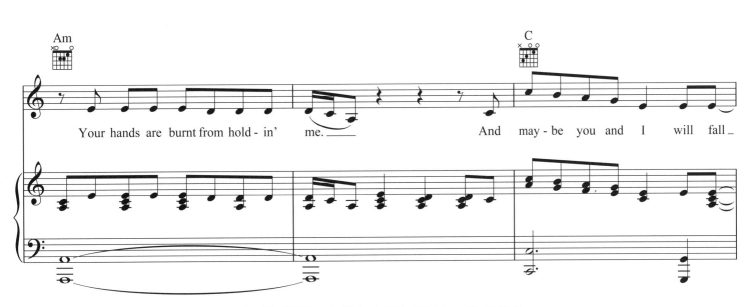

WAR PAINT

Words and Music by JOLEEN BELLE,
NOLAN LAMBROZA and JULIA MICHAELS

Face to face, but miles a - way. Build - ing trench -
Scar to scar, I wan - na know

es out of emp - ty space. Lay here next to me,
ry that you nev - er told. Don't shut me out, don't think too much.

en - close the dis - tance in be - tween. I'll take off
Don't keep that bar - ri - cade up.

Recorded a half step lower.

DANCE WITH ME

Words and Music by
DAN ROCKETT

NOSTALGIC

Words and Music by JUSTIN TRANTER,
DAN KEYES, VAUGHN OLIVER
and RYLAND BLACKINTON

Don't be sad ____
I won - der ____

____ that it's o - ver. Just be hap - py that it hap-pened to us.
____ if you're wear - in' that gold chain with a prom - ise from me.

E-ven though we lost it, ___ I still get nos - tal - gic, nos - tal - gic. ___

GOOD GOES THE BYE

Words and Music by SHANE McANALLY,
JIMMY ROBBINS and NATALIE HEMBY

Moderately

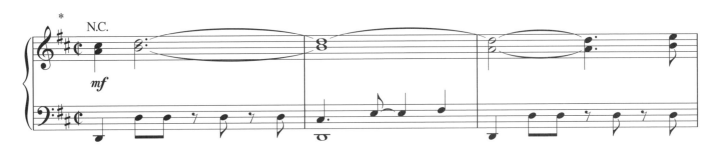

They say Rome__ was-n't

built in a day,__ but you__ and I went and built it an-y-way.__ And it on-

* Recorded a half step lower.

92

BAD REPUTATION

Words and Music by KELLY CLARKSON,
KELLY SHEEHAN, BONNIE McKEE
and GREG KURSTIN

Moderately

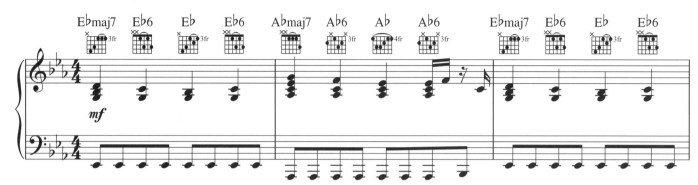

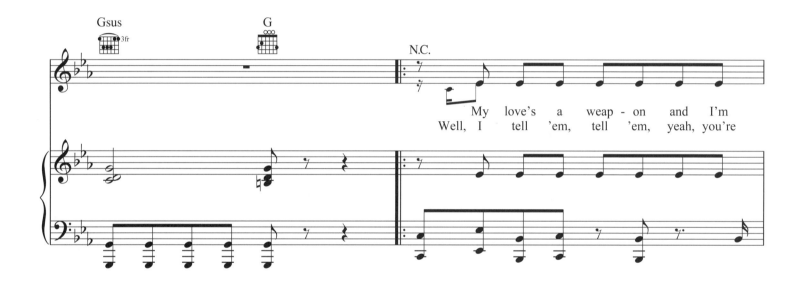

My love's a weap-on and I'm
Well, I tell 'em, tell 'em, yeah, you're

knock-in' 'em dead. __ I got a heart __ as tough as leath-er, get what I want __
noth-in' to me. __ I tell 'em that you, __ you're just an-oth-er, you're just __

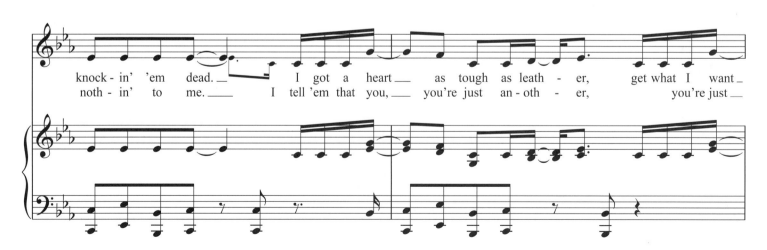

IN THE BLUE

Words and Music by KELLY CLARKSON,
ANJULIE PERSAUD, FRANSISCA HALL
and JESSE SHATKIN

SECOND WIND

Words and Music by CHRIS DESTEFANO,
SHANE McANALLY and MAREN MORRIS